THE
TARXIEN TEMPLES
Tarxien

ANTHONY PACE

PHOTOGRAPHY
DANIEL CILIA

HERITAGE BOOKS
IN ASSOCIATION WITH

H Heritage Malta
2006

HOW TO GET TO TARXIEN TEMPLES

By bus:
Bus Nos. 1, 2, 3, 4, 6, 8, 11, 12,13, 15, 17, 18, 19, 20, 21, 26, 27, 28, 29, 30 and 115 from Valletta bus terminus stopping at Paola main square (De Paule Square). Walk along Church Avenue straight up to Neolithic Temples Street.

By car:
Main roads leading to Paola. As you enter Paolo, just before the parish church, turn left into Church Avenue. Drive straight past Boffa Square, which is in front of the School. As you approach Pace Grazzo Football Ground, turn right into Neolithic Temples Street.

Tarxien Temples
Neolithic Temples Street
Tarxien PLA 11
Malta
Tel: 2169 5578
www.heritagemalta.org

Insight Heritage Guides Series No: 12
General Editor: Louis J. Scerri

Published by Heritage Books, a subsidiary of Midsea Books Ltd, Carmelites Street, Sta Venera HMR 11, Malta
sales@midseabooks.com

Insight Heritage Guides is a series of books intended to give an insight into aspects and sites of Malta's rich heritage, culture and traditions.

Produced by Mizzi Design & Graphic Services
Printed by Gutenberg Press

Editorial © Heritage Books
Literary © Anthony Pace
Photography © Daniel Cilia

First published 2006

ISBN: 99932-7-078-4

THE TARXIEN TEMPLES

The megalithic temple complex of Tarxien was constructed at the height of Malta's Late Neolithic period, on a site that was used over a span of several millennia. The site appears to have first been used as early as the Żebbuġ phase (beginning c.4100 BC). The megalithic character of the site emerged as early as 3600 BC, reaching a highly complex layout by about 3000 BC. This period was one of continued architectural expansion and of artistic flowering on a scale that marked the entire Maltese archipelago. Existing buildings were redesigned, extended, and embellished with remarkable megalithic art. During the Early Bronze Age (after 2500 BC) the Tarxien temples entered an important new phase. Its spaces and walls were now used for funerary purposes, with striking new rituals being introduced. The elegant chambers of the temples became part crematorium and part cemetery. Later still, the site appears to have been used during Phoenician, Punic, and Roman times. Clearly, Malta's very limited geographic resources meant that strategic locations retained their importance from one generation to another.

The Tarxien temples are, therefore, an important source of information. Their value lies in the wealth of relics and traces of the past that have been transmitted down to our generation. Tarxien still provides one of the most comprehensive repertoire of prehistoric art that allows us to gain important insights into one of the Mediterranean's lost civilizations. The scientific value of the site was recognized by Sir Temi Zammit, the father of Maltese archaeology and excavator of the monument. The discovery of Tarxien was epoch-making in many ways. From the beginning, the remains of the temple complex were destined to become a world attraction for scholars and travellers. The monument is still one of the most frequently visited locations on the islands. In more recent times, the Tarxien temples were included on UNESCO's World Heritage List, in recognition of the monument's important place in the history of world architecture. Finally, another important aspect of the temples of Ħal Tarxien is the fact that, increasingly, the monument is steadily gaining importance as a national icon of sorts. Whether through its art works, or the fact that it forms part of a broader repertoire of megalithic monuments, the Tarxien temple complex is distinctive enough to capture community sentiments and, therefore, holds a special place in the creation of Maltese identity.

A FEW STONES COME TO LIGHT ...

The ruins of the Tarxien temples as they gradually emerged during the first few weeks of excavation. At a very early stage, Sir Temi Zammit was confronted by irrefutable remains of apses and the prospect of a unique scientific discovery

It was in many ways an age of discovery that saw the Tarxien temples come to light during the first few years of the twentieth century. This period in the history of Maltese archaeology was a seminal one. It opened rather dramatically in 1902 with the discovery of the Ħal Saflieni Hypogeum, located less than a kilometre to the west of Tarxien. Up till then, the idea of prehistory had not yet caught on as a very popular or academic area of interest. The slow dissemination of knowledge about international discoveries meant that even important comparative studies could not be undertaken by scholars working in different parts of the world. The idea that humankind had an ancient past that was much older than history itself, was still relatively alien one to the popular reader. Hominind fossil discoveries and other prehistoric finds

encountered during the nineteenth century were very often held in doubt. Their antiquity and authenticity were questioned. Megalithic buildings were simply thought of as ruins of former refined buildings of classical antiquity. At the time, the impact of Greek, Egyptian, and Near Eastern antiquities on western imagination was still tremendous and extensive. It was, therefore, not unusual for received wisdom to associate antiquities with classical, biblical, or Near Eastern civilizations.

In Malta, nearly all known antiquities were, for instance, ascribed to Phoenician, Punic, Roman, Early Christian, and later periods. The study of Maltese history thus came to revolve around a sequential framework in which Phoenician and classical antiquity were seen to have been disrupted by an Islamic interval prior to a Christian revival that culminated with the arrival of the crusading Order of St John. By 1900, very few scholars dated the Maltese temples to prehistory. Indeed, even the very idea of a time before history as ever having existed beyond biblical narratives, was too novel a concept to be readily accepted. For the most part, ideas of a pre-Phoenician past were firmly grounded in mythology and legends. When 'rude stone monuments' failed to fit in with any class of known classical civilization, it would not have been unusual for prehistoric monuments to be seen as products of giants or cyclopean endeavours. It was during the opening decades of the twentieth century that the first syntheses of world prehistory began to appear in scholarly circles and academic institutions.

The discovery of the Ħal Saflieni Hypogeum in 1902 began to change all this. Ħal Saflieni simply pushed Malta's antiquity back by several centuries. A year before, the Germany scholar Albert Mayr, published a first detailed description of Malta's megaliths which were ascribed to a prehistoric period. Ħal Saflieni fortified this view, so that, quite suddenly, Malta 'possessed' a prehistory. At the time, the academic world was still very much under the spell of the great discoveries. Schlieman's excavations at Troy, undertaken between 1871 and 1873, were still fresh in popular imagination. At the same time as the discovery and excavation of Ħal Saflieni and the Tarxien temples, Sir Temi Zammit's contemporary, Sir Arthur Evans, undertook excavations at Knossos. Another famous contemporary of the time, Howard Carter, began his prospecting in the Valley of the Kings which, in 1922, led to the discovery of Tutankhamun's tomb.

The Hypogeum attracted a great deal of public and scholarly attention. Nineteenth-century political and administrative developments linked to the protection of antiquities drove the colonial authorities to undertake much-needed reforms. One of the first steps was the establishment of a 'Museum Department' under the care and management of a special committee. Sir Themistocles Zammit, medical practitioner and researcher, a well-known personality and a keen student of antiquities, was appointed curator of the museum. Apart from creating a scientific collection and display, Zammit also embarked on a series of field campaigns with the aim of discovering and excavating as many archaeological sites as possible. The creation of the museum and the steady identification of hitherto-unknown monuments, must have

Temi Zammit's excavation provided the first stratigraphic sequence of Maltese prehistoric antiquities. The chronology of Maltese prehistory has since been refined, and will no doubt be subject to further refinements as a result of future research

The internal features of the Tarxien temples were gradually revealed as layer after layer of soil and debris were removed by Temi Zammit's workforce

created greater public interest. Often, topographic peculiarities such as stone heaps, megaliths, isolated ashlar stones, soil colour, and unusual cuts in the rock surfaces were enough to give an indication of archaeological remains. Being acutely aware of the importance of understanding the local landscape, Zammit toured the islands, always keeping an open mind to casual references to reports of unusual features that farmers often mentioned.

The Museum Annual Reports are full of references to various reports of discoveries by different people coming from all walks of life. Clearly, the general public was steadily becoming more aware of the importance of certain antiquities, a factor that was to play a significant role in the discovery and protection of monuments during the first decades of the twentieth

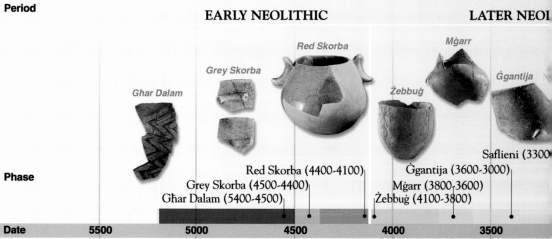

CHRONOLOGY OF MALTESE PREHISTORY BASED ON CALIBRATED CARBON

Period

EARLY NEOLITHIC   LATER NEOL

Red Skorba

Mġarr

Grey Skorba

Ġgantija

Għar Dalam

Żebbuġ

Saflieni (3300

Phase

Red Skorba (4400-4100)
Grey Skorba (4500-4400)
Għar Dalam (5400-4500)

Ġgantija (3600-3000)
Mġarr (3800-3600)
Żebbuġ (4100-3800)

Date	5500	5000	4500	4000	3500

PYRAMI

century. Indeed, it was such a report that led Sir Temi Zammit to Tarxien in 1913. A field tenant had casually informed Sir Temi that he often used to come across large stones just a few feet below the surface soils of his fields. Zammit visited these field, which he found to be a few metres away from the nearby 'Tal-Erwieħ' cemetery. Similar stones had also been encountered when foundation trenches were dug for the small chapel of the cemetery. Later, Zammit noted other odd features. One particular tract of land in the area, referred to as 'Tal-Bajjada', possibly referring to its light-coloured soil, was quite distinct and conspicuous. Close by, there stood a heap of stone debris, which went by the name of 'Tal-Borġ' (*heap*). Were the different soil colours and stone debris signs of what may have been buried in the field?

In 1913, Zammit could do very little about the Tarxien report. At the time he was still occupied with work at the Hypogeum. A few years before, his colleague Father Manwel Magri, the Hypogeum's first excavator, had passed away leaving the Hypogeum work unfinished. This work had to be concluded before new discoveries could be addressed.

Zammit decided to proceed with full-scale excavations of Tarxien in 1915. Work began in July and continued up to September of that year. The field known as 'Tal-Bajjada' was the primary objective of Zammit's work. A trench was cut in the middle of the field. Stone blocks immediately came to light a few centimetres below the soil. The trench was extended with stone after stone being uncovered. Before long, the familiar sight of large stone apses, already known from Ħaġar Qim, Mnajdra, and Ġgantija, stood out. After a few days of digging, the ruins of a prehistoric building could be seen. The magnitude of the discovery was not lost upon Zammit. Here were the unmistakable remains of an unexcavated prehistoric temple and, therefore, a discovery of significant scientific importance. Like the discovery of the Hypogeum, the excavation of the Tarxien temples was an epoch-making undertaking.

Decades after Zammit's work, the Tarxien temples continue to yield important information. The occupation of the site on which the temples now stand appears to be older than the megalithic version that can now be seen on site. So far, we know that the earliest pottery gathered from

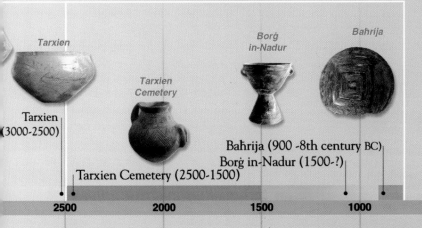

BRONZE AGE

Tarxien

Tarxien
(3000-2500)

Tarxien
Cemetery

Tarxien Cemetery (2500-1500)

Borġ
in-Nadur

Baħrija

Baħrija (900 -8th century BC)
Borġ in-Nadur (1500-?)

| 2500 | 2000 | 1500 | 1000 | 500 |

CRETE   STONEHENGE

Rounded to nearest calibrated Radiocarbon dates

the site, belongs to the Żebbuġ Phase (4100-3800 BC). This period marked the beginning of what is often referred to as the 'Temple period'. The term itself is only a generic reference to a distinct period during which the inhabitants of the Maltese islands constructed a series of imposing megalithic buildings in various parts of the archipelago. The period itself can easily be referred to by the term 'Late Neolithic'. Judging from the extent and elaborate nature of the Tarxien temples, one could imagine that the site may have once been held in high esteem by the islanders. As a monumental site, the Tarxien temples experienced a number of transformations with building after building being added or altered, no doubt in response to changing social needs.

The first version of a megalithic structure, Tarxien FE, was built some time during the Ġgantija phase (c. 3600 BC). In comparison to the other main buildings of the site, Tarxien FE is a modest affair. Very little is left of this building; which appears to be reminiscent of Ta' Ħaġrat temple (Mġarr, Malta). It seems that building alterations continued with numerous interventions being made over a number of years. No one knows the length of time that was required for the completion of these alterations. One can only guess, keeping in mind that, for example, the Romanesque and Gothic cathedrals of Europe took centuries to complete. The Maltese temples are, of course, buildings of a much smaller scale and may have in fact taken less time to build. Although impressive and in places utilizing large megaliths, the Maltese temples are not too overwhelming in scale and mass. Given the right organization of sufficient resources, some of the

temples could have easily been built during one dry season.

The Tarxien temples were soon enlarged with a major building spree taking place during the Tarxien Phase (3000-2500 BC). It was during this period that the entire site was altered with the three major buildings that are now visible, being constructed in their present location. Elsewhere in the ancient world, nothing comparable was being built in stone in lands located within a short distance from Malta. Nearby Sicily appears to have remained oblivious to Malta's megalithic phenomenon, in spite of contacts and sea travel. The same can be said of Sardinia and the Italian mainland. The Aegean was also following its own particular evolution, with the appearance of the palace civilization, especially on Crete.

The chequered history of the Tarxien temples entered an unexpected phase during the Bronze Age. Around 2500 BC, parts of the temple complex were used as a cremation cemetery. Temple architecture may have no longer held the same significance that it did centuries before. If megalithic monuments were built at all, these became significantly smaller and almost inconspicuous in the landscape, in comparison to the Late Neolithic temples. It was only at this juncture in the history of world civilization that the 'palace civilization' on Crete appeared. Likewise, the Great Pyramids were built on the Giza plateau, and the megalithic version of Stonehenge was completed in Britain.

The Maltese megalithic phenomenon remained very much a world on to its own, but it predated much later wonders of the archaeological world by well over a millennium.

The complexity of the Tarxien temples is best understood through aerial photography, a view afforded only in modern times. Prehistoric ground level perspectives provided a different experience: interiors may seemed more secluded and labyrinthal

INSIDE THE MONUMENTS

The current setting and approach to the Tarxien temples does not reflect much of the original prehistoric landscape. The temples are situated in a large hollow, surrounded on all sides by modern buildings. Centuries of land use and field building for agricultural purposes meant that even the most imposing monuments could easily fall out of use and become buried. The Tarxien temple complex is, in fact, one of the unusual examples of a Maltese prehistoric building that had been completely covered by earth and debris. The transformation of the landscape is one of the least appreciated aspects in

the history of humankind. When Sir Temi Zammit first excavated the site, the protection of the monument was paramount in his mind. Excavation meant that the exposed ruins ended up being surrounded by fields that now towered above the ancient buildings. Originally Sir Temi Zammit had made sure that these fields would be retained as a protective buffer zone around the Tarxien temples. Sadly, almost all of these fields have since been developed, with modern buildings soaring above the temples. Because of this, the Tarxien temples have become divorced from their landscape. Natural skylines that

once played such an important role in the location, design, and building of the temples are now completely obliterated from view.

Arguably, the Tarxien temples are the most complex of Malta's megalithic structures in terms of layout and internal embellishments. The temple compound grew beyond its original humble beginnings that can still be seen in the remains of Tarxien FE. But, at its heyday, the site encompassed a number of buildings that had been constructed organically in response to changing requirements. The building and engineering techniques used throughout the development of the compound were among the most sophisticated. In addition, the Tarxien temples also became a repository

of some of the most important art works that were created during Mediterranean prehistory.

The temple compound now comprises four major building units, referred to as Tarxien Far East (Tarxien FE), Tarxien South, Tarxien East, and Tarxien Central. The buildings experienced a number of changes throughout the Maltese Later Neolithic (3600-2500 BC). Different parts of the compound were later used as a cremation cemetery during the Early Bronze Age (2500-1500 BC).

Restored conical stone cup on a stand with signs of fire in the cup

THE DISCOVERY OF THE TARXIEN TEMPLES

A large stone bowl found in Tarxien Central prior to reconstruction

First noted in 1913, the Tarxien temples were first excavated in the summer of 1915. This first major phase of excavations continued during the summer of 1916. The effects of the World War of 1914-18, then raging across the European mainland, soon began to have ripple effects on the Maltese islands. The Tarxien excavations were put on hold, with work being taken up again during 1917 and 1918, in spite of some funding difficulties. Excavations were concluded in 1919.

During the 1915 and 1916 campaigns, the major excavation works concentrated on the exposure of the central and south temples of the Tarxien temple complex. In addition, Zammit published the first scientific reports, in which he outlined the importance of the site for Maltese archaeology. Zammit's excavations provided the first conceptual framework for understanding Maltese prehistory. In addition to Neolithic layers, the excavations yielded later deposits that belonged to the Bronze Age. The temple also yielded one of the most remarkable repertoires of artworks known from world prehistory. This repertoire still attracts a great deal of scientific attention. The Tarxien temples also served as a pioneering laboratory for testing restoration work. Zammit used the principle of capping damaged megalithic walls and surviving foundation walls with rubble or dry-stone walling. By 1919, the prehistoric temples assumed much of the character that is so familiar today.

The facade of Tarxien South, with the partial reconstruction of the entrance

Opposite page: The first apse of Tarxien South shortly after excavation

The altars in the first apse of Tarxien South. Notice the amount of stone 'cones'

During the campaigns of 1917, 1918, and 1919 the Eastern temples, including the earliest temple on the site, were excavated. In 1929, Thomas Ashby undertook excavations aimed at understanding the chronological relationship between the various units of the temple complex. Later excavations by John Evans in 1954 and David Trump in 1958 revisited Ashby's work. During 1997 the Museums Department excavated a trial trench near the old site museum. An apse was discovered and examined before being covered for protection purposes. Other work by the Museums Department was undertaken, during 2001, in the western innermost apse of Tarxien East. This part of the building had, in 1999, experienced a collapse precisely at a point that had already been restored by Zammit during his excavations.

TARXIEN FAR EAST

When first built, Tarxien FE was designed as a five-apse building. The remains of this building suggest that the structure was originally small in comparison to other temples. The eastern half of this temple has not survived at all. A number of factors may have contributed towards this disturbance. For instance, having been built of small boulders, a technique also used at Ta' Ħaġrat (Mġarr, Malta) and Kordin, Tarxien FE may have had far

less chances of survival. Looking at the later buildings on the site, a different style of masonry will be immediately noticed. Here, accomplished quarrying and rock-cutting meant that later megaliths were better formed. This technique ensured better structural stability and improved chances of survival through a system of inter-fitting megaliths. In Maltese megalithic architecture, the use of larger stones was the key to achieving an almost permanent presence. The extent of the disturbance in Tarxien FE may have also been due to quarrying, or the re-utilization of stone after the original structure had fallen out of use. Yet again, the disappearance of the eastern portion of this small temple may have been linked to the cutting of a large pit, just off-centre to the main passageway of this small temple. There are no clear views as to the purpose of the hollow. Some scholars have suggested that it may have once served as a tomb, but burial grounds are not normally associated with temples. It may also have been a votive pit or a space meant for storage.

In design, Tarxien FE is similar to Ġgantija S and Ħaġar Qim N, also five-apse buildings. But unlike these two well-known buildings, Tarxien FE is much smaller in proportion. The main passageway of the temple measures just over 10m in length, from the entrance to the inner apse. Like many of the other contemporary temple buildings, Tarxien FE was designed and constructed with a concave façade. The entrance to the building was placed in the centre of this façade. The main entrance to the building led into a central passageway which is aligned roughly due south.

The innermost point of the temple is marked by a central apse. According to David Trump, this feature suggests

that Tarxien FE may have followed an early design. The main axis of the passageway is paved by a series of stone slabs, a feature that is found in many of the Maltese temples. Access into the main passageway was marked by a raised threshold, which can still be seen today. In certain places within the temple, one encounters patches of *torba* (beaten earth), evidence that the apses were in the most part paved with compact earth containing small stones and fragments of pottery. More often than not, *torba* appears to have been use to pave apses; flag stones, were used mainly in central passageways.

A small stone niche with spindlewhorls or phalli. It was found close to the Oracle hole V

A sherd from the western field at Tarxien. The top is the lip of a pot. The decoration represents a bird modelled in between cattle horns

A clay sherd with modelled heads and an animal (a hog?) on top

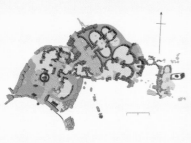

SHIP GRAFFITI

Even today, after several millennia of sea travel and exploration, the sea remains one of humankind's challenges. In ancient times, seafaring was a dangerous experiment which may not necessarily have had a happy ending. The loss of small precarious sea craft was a common occurrence. The loss of life without any news and the perils of prolonged travel at the mercy of the sea became the very stuff of legend and myth. The appearance of sea craft, a rare occasion, would have been an event in itself. The Tarxien ship graffiti, thought to date to the Early Bronze Age if not to an earlier period, are a reminder of the presence of the sea in the life of islanders. The carved icons may reflect types of sea craft that had for centuries been in use in the eastern Mediterranean, especially the Aegean. Are the Tarxien ship graffiti a record of successful journeys by farmers who doubled up as sailors? Or are they a document of the eventful arrival of a foreign fleet?

TARXIEN SOUTH

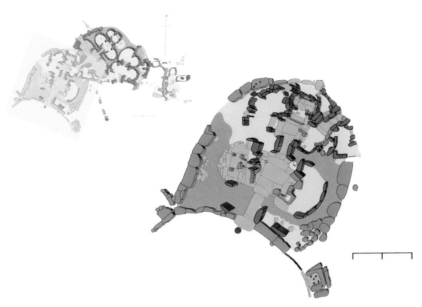

Stone rollers often thought of as being possibly associated with the transport of megaliths, or at another extreme, with rituals or other culturally-related activities

The modern-reconstructed entrance to Tarxien South

Tarxien South was one of the major temples that were constructed during the Tarxien phase (3000-2500 BC). More than any other temple period building, Tarxien South was distinguished by a series of rock carvings that to this day make up one of the most important repertoires of art works known from world prehistory. The complex arrangement of Tarxien South was unequalled in other parts of the temple compound which did not appear to have had the same level of elaborate embellishments. The importance of Tarxien South appears to have evolved over time, as alterations to the building were made.

Tarxien South was originally designed to a four-apse plan. The extensive restoration works that took place after the excavations of 1915 and 1916 actually highlight some of the important alterations that had been made to the original layout of the temple during prehistory. The precise extent of these changes

The complex arrangement of the first apses of Tarxien South. The chambers were dominated by a monumental statue, altars, and a series of rock-carved representations of animals, spiral motifs and other abstract patterns. The language of this art has not yet been deciphered

Throughout the temple, tethering holes were carved in strategic megaliths, especially those that formed doorways. The holes may have been part of a securing mechanism to close access ways

still needs to be clarified by future research. In some cases, changes may have been intentional. Others may have been accidental. It is also still very difficult to establish whether all of these changes actually took place at the same time, or whether they were separated by generations of development. The first, and most extensive of these changes, concerned the monumental entrance and walls of the western apses. Visitors will notice that these architectural features are reconstructions which now rest on top of prehistoric foundations that were discovered by Zammit during the excavation of the site. One problem with reconstructions is that although often very useful as interpretive tools, they can often distort important aspects of the past. For instance the reconstructions in Tarxien South, strongly suggest that, some time during the past, almost all of the walls of the western half of this building had been

intentionally dismantled. The reasons for this are unknown and it is not sure whether these changes actually occurred during prehistory or during later times. However, it is probable that the western portion of the building would have been more of an open space, rather than enclosed apses. Today the practice of conservation and restoration discourages reconstruction on archaeological sites and monuments because of the ambiguities that such modern reconstructions often create.

The second important alteration in Tarxien S concern the innermost eastern apse, **7**. This side apse was altered to serve as a link between Tarxien South and the newly-built Tarxien Central. This transitory space also served to house a number of niches, some of which can still be seen today. Tarxien South was built on a different axis, a slight re-alignment from the orientation of Tarxien FE. The significance of this change in orientation is not quite clear. For instance, it may have been linked to the open space that had been created by the dismantling of the western wall, if the latter had in fact occurred during prehistory.

The reconstructed gateway now hides most of the interiors of the apses. As a rule, main entrances were located in the centre of a concave façade. The original entrance may have created a similar effect. Original doorways are relatively narrow and consist of a classic trilithon made of two upright megaliths and capped by a horizontal lintel. Standing outside of the temple, visitors have a good view of what awaits them inside the building. The immediate vista afforded by this arrangement is that of the innermost point of the building, in this case an elaborate niche built on a platform. This may have been the intended effect of the temple builders. The narrow doorway would have also provided additional structural strength to the building.

The temple façade therefore served as a windowless curtain that protected the interior of the building. The narrow entrance served to filter links between the external world and the internal temple spaces. The link between the sacred and the non-sacred, or the exclusive and the non-exclusive, was managed through narrow entrances.

On entering the temple itself, the perspective suddenly changes. Just within the doorway, visitors stand in the main passageway of the building. The passageway, **1**, is paved with flagstones, suggesting that the space may have originally doubled up as a small courtyard, and may have therefore meant to be roofless. Standing in this court, visitors encounter a remarkable arrangement

COLOSSAL STATUE

The colossal statue from Tarxien is remarkable because of its sheer size. The statue appears to be the oldest monumental anthropomorphic representation known from Mediterranean prehistory. Originally, the statue represented a figure that was draped in a carved pleated costume. It is thought to have once stood at a height of almost two metres. Its location, close to the entrance of Tarxien South, was strategic probably to command the attention of all who entered the buildings. The iconography of prominent figures, whether a deity or community leader, was executed in a size that adequately reflected the status of the represented personage. The colossal statue follows a style that was reproduced in several other smaller statues discovered at Tarxien. The original colossal statue of Tarxien has been moved indoors from its original location.

A unique feature of Tarxien South was an elaborately decorated altar, consisting of a mensa and a niche that reflected the typical enclosed trilithon structure known from various Maltese temples. The altar's mensa was a originally a single megalithic stone block that had been hollowed out to serve as an enclosed receptacle in which a number of flint blades and animal bones were placed

of carved stones, standing megaliths, altars, and a very distinctive statue of a human figure. The location, number, and concentration of these sculpted elements in a relatively small space is a reflection of the importance that was attached to this particular area of the temple compound. The decorative elements are unified by similar sculpting techniques and the general appearance of the stone. The recurring use of spirals and spiral-derived patterns are also a strong unifying theme. However, on closer inspection, the two apses of Tarxien South are also quite different in content.

The eastern apse, **2**, appears to have been dedicated to activities linked to the colossal statue that is located immediately on the boundary that separates this apse from the passageway. The figure, often referred to by some scholars and enthusiasts as a 'mother goddess', is a large-scale rendering of a form of statuary that was widespread during the temple period. The statuary may have represented a deity or an esteemed person. It is believed that, originally, the Tarxien statue

may have stood as much as 2m high, making it one of the oldest large-scale monumental statues known from world prehistory.

Accompanying this colossal statue is a very distinctive-looking altar. This consists of a hollowed square megalith, which served as the altar's mensa, on which stands a niche, made of finely-carved rectangular stones. The front of the *mensa* is decorated with spirals set out in two tiers. The altar has an interesting story. When first encountered in 1915 during the excavation of the site, the altar was found to be hollow. Zammit surmised that the altar was meant to be a receptacle. As more rubble was cleared, it soon became evident that a hole cut in the front face of the *mensa* provided access to the interior of the altar. The hole was blocked by a stone plug that had been carefully sealed by small stone wedges. These seals had not been removed since prehistory. Inside, the contents of the altar comprised sheep and ox bones, as well as a quantity of marine shells. A long bone spatula and thirteen flint flakes were also discovered. The deposit also contained numerous fragments of pottery. When the plug was first removed by Sir Temi Zammit, the first item to be encountered within was a four- and-a-half inch stone knife. This knife would have been the last item to be placed inside the altar before the plug was sealed. The event was never to be repeated until well over four millennia later!

A series of low-lying carved stones, decorated with 'wave' patterns, provides a unifying theme as well as a threshold that separates the inner parts of the apse from the paved court. The apse itself is paved with *torba*. The wall of the apse comprises many of the original megaliths. The tops of these stones were damaged, probably

intentionally or as a result of more recent quarrying.

By contrast, the western apse, **3**, comprises a curious arrangement of altars, standing stones, and low-lying relief sculptures. The apse was originally semi-circular in form but, unlike its eastern counterpart, it was found to be missing its entire wall. The technique of using small stones, dry-stone walling, distinguishes the wall from original megalithic ones. As explained earlier, it may be that the original walls had been removed during prehistory in response to new ritual requirements. If this had indeed been the case, was the removal of the walls linked to a possible concern with building alignments? Was this apse re-shaped to function as an open platform on which decorated megaliths and altars were given prominence? Was Tarxien South transformed into a more public area of the temple compound? Were the changes made in Tarxien South compensated by the building of Tarxien Central?

The arrangement of the decorated megaliths is also very interesting. First, it is noticeable that the apse is distinguished from the temple's main passage way by two low-lying megaliths. These stones, measuring just under 2 metres in length, about 90cm in width and 50cm in height, are beautifully cut and each is decorated with a two-tier design of spirals. Interestingly, the stone blocks were positioned so as to replicate the idea of a concave temple façade. A similar arrangement seems to have been used in the Ġgantija temples. A paved passageway, left between the stone blocks, leads into the interior of the apse. The passageway is marked by a semi-circular threshold.

The passageway is flanked by two upright stones. In 1956, ship graffiti were noticed on the faces of these two very important megaliths. The significance of these graffiti is important to the history of Mediterranean maritime archaeology and history. In general,

On entering Tarxien South, visitors encounter a series of spiral-decorated megaliths and upright stones to the left of the main passage way. The decorated megaliths mark a boundary and define the entrance to the interior of an apse. The arrangement echoes a typical temple façade. Within the apse lie a series of decorated stones. Two of these have carved rows of farm animals – sheep, goats and pigs, the staple Neolithic meat source. The two uprights flanking the entrance were marked with a number of sea-craft graffiti

Images of sea-craft were carved on the two upright megaliths seen in the forefront. These graffiti are thought to be among the oldest known in the Central and western Mediterranean

the iconography of temple period Malta does not inform us much about maritime activities in spite of the inhabitants being surrounded by sea. In fact, the Tarxien ship graffiti are the only known images of sea-craft known from Maltese prehistory. For some scholars, these graffiti represent one of the earliest records of sea-craft known from central and western Mediterranean prehistory. The images conjure quite a number of intriguing questions. Were the ships carved during the temple period? Or are they of a later Bronze Age date? What do the stones represent? Are they a record of a unique event, the arrival of a fleet? Do the graffiti represent a history of various sea crossings?

Within the interior of the apse, Zammit came across a number of stones, decorated with finely-carved images of spirals, plant-like motifs, as well as depictions of animals.

The remaining areas of Tarxien South again show signs of substantial remodelling. Apse **5**, also located on the western side of the building, was extensively reconstructed, the walls of the chamber being built of modern dry stone-walling. The entrance to the apse is marked by a few upright megaliths which appear to be in situ. The floor is paved with hard earth, giving the chamber a less-refined appearance in comparison to the two outer chambers of the temple. Tucked away to the extreme right, in the chamber's interior, is a niche built of slabs. The position of the niche is somewhat unusual, owing mainly to the deformed plan of the apse. This deformity may in part be the result of the modern reconstruction, although the building of the central elevated niche on the main axis of the temple may have also contributed to the unusual plan of the chamber. Interestingly, the niche was found to contain several bones and horns of cattle, sheep, and goats. The parallel with the hollow decorated altar near the colossal statue is intriguing. Almost like trophies, certain animal parts may have played an important role in the day-to-day life of the temples.

The corresponding apse built opposite chamber **5**, apse **7**, lost its former plan following extensive alterations. The apse was divided into a narrow passage-way leading to Tarxien Central and a small structure. Of the latter, only the stumps of a small porthole entrance such as the two found in the outer apses of Hagar Qim, have survived. Almost opposite these porthole stumps lies a small chamber which is distinguished by a single stone entrance of the type known from the interior chambers of Mnajdra. Within the Tarxien example, and to the right of the entrance, lie several

recesses formed by an arrangement of slabs. During excavation, Zammit found that, as in the case of the niche in apse **5**, these recesses were packed with animal bones. Animal horn-cores were very conspicuous, as were a number of stone mortars, cones, and two triangular stone objects (one of them pierced) which have often been described as weights by Zammit. The function of such secluded chambers is unclear, but the persistent presence of stacked animal bones would suggest the possibility of a store of ritual-related animal remains.

Finally, the other prominent structure in Tarxien South is the raised platform and niche located on the main axis of the temple, in between apses **5** and **7**. The whole arrangement of this imposing feature is very particular. The raised platform, which is about 60cm high above the floor of the temple, is not unlike a theatrical stage. The front of the platform has a distinguished appearance, consisting of a large megalith decorated with a two-tier spiral design pattern. The top of the platform is paved with stone slabs. What was the function of this platform and the raised niche? Unfortunately, archaeology does not normally enable us to capture the essence of non-material aspects of ritual or social gatherings, such as ceremonies or performances. Such aspects include a certain degree of theatrical expression. The Tarxien example may have been designed to provide a clear vista of proceedings and of the central niche.

The back walls of Tarxien South were restored in dry-stone walling after the site was excavated between 1915 and 1919

THE OLDEST FREE-STANDING MONUMENTS OF THE WORLD

The development of scientific dating techniques ushered in a new era in the study of archaeology. Radiocarbon dating, a discovery related to atomic research, has captured popular imagination, primarily because of the impact that it had during the post-World War II decades and the 1970s. The first radiocarbon dates questioned many of the established chronologies of world prehistory. The prehistory of places such as Malta was often considered as being related to that of other older regions. Carbon dating changed all this.

As a result of Prof. Colin Renfrew's work on the recalibration of pioneering carbon dates, Maltese prehistory was shown to be older than previously thought. One of the biggest surprises that met students of Maltese prehistory was the fact that the archipelago's megalithic temples were much older than Stonehenge, the palace of Knossos, or the great Egyptian pyramids. According to Prof. Renfrew, carbon dating suggests that the Maltese temples are in fact the 'oldest free-standing stone monuments' known from world prehistory.

TARXIEN CENTRAL

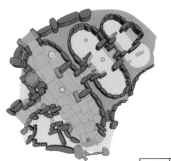

Aerial view of Tarxien Central. Walking through the building, the interiors give the impression of a labyrinth-like arrangement of rooms, passage-ways, and niches. From the air, the layout of the Tarxien temples reflect a complex arrangement of symmetrically-planned spaces. This symmetry reflects an acute sense of order and design

In comparison to mainstream layouts of Malta's megalithic temples, Tarxien Central is a class on to its own. Uniquely, Tarxien Central is made up of six apses, rather than the customary four or five. The temple still follows basic engineering principles used elsewhere on the island. But Tarxien Central also exhibits a more refined use of stone which clearly entailed sophisticated quarrying, refined stone-dressing, and highly-developed building techniques. As with many of Maltese temple interiors, one experiences a play on principal axis, secluded areas, public areas, and transitory spaces.

The main axis of Tarxien Central is dominated by a low-lying stone slab which is distinctively decorated with two large spirals. A copy now stands instead off the original which was removed for protection purposes. The effect of the slab may have been both symbolic and functional. The slab requires visitors to climb over the

The 'oculus' motif, suggested by the two spirals carved on a low-lying stone. Did this bar entrance into the inner reaches of the temple? (Stone is a copy of the original)

Left: East view of Tarxien South. The reddish hue and the cracks in the stone are signs of burning, possibly dating back to the Early Bronze when the temples were used as a cremation cemetery

The hearth

stone, should they wish to enter the innermost areas of the temple. The spirals added more significance to the function of this intentional obstacle. Some scholars believe that the two large spirals may have represented a charmed oculus, to ward off undesired intruders. Indeed, the entire Tarxien temple compound gives the impression that segregation or differentiation may have been a prominent element in the day-to-day business of these imposing buildings. Alternatively, one can think of this careful partitioning of space as a way of defining the different functions of individual interior spaces of a building.

The two outer apses of Tarxien Central, **10** and **12**, present a spectacle of stonework. The right-hand apse was also modified by the insertion of a doorway. The general plan of the two apses is of particular interest. The chambers follow very wide curves so that, together, they appear to form a single space. The space is paved all over not by thin stone slabs but by well-shaped megaliths. The use of these megaliths may have been intended as a levelling measure. But their overall function seems to have been that of providing a stone surface for the area's floor, a solution which also helped water drainage, especially during rainy seasons. The paving slabs may delineate areas that were not covered by a permanent roof. This is further supported by the presence of a hearth in the middle of the area. The hearth, which still shows signs of burning, would have required good ventilation when in use.

The megaliths of the area are exceptionally well-formed, a sign of accomplished quarrying techniques and refined stone dressing. Such

THE TARXIEN TEMPLES

techniques enabled the builders of Tarxien Central to lay megaliths in a well-fitting arrangement, which is not unlike the use of ashlar masonry. The ravishes of time and the signs of burning have left an impact on the stones, but one can still admire the refined quality of craftsmanship that once shaped these majestic stones. The stonework is even more remarkable when one considers that no metal tools are known from the temple period!

What was the function of these two large chambers? The space may have served as a transitory one and, possibly, a more accessible one used for assemblies and gatherings. To the left of the main axis, in apse **10** stands a large bowl that had been carved entirely out of a single stone block. The exact purpose of this bowl is unknown, although many scholars favour the idea that it may have served for votive offerings. Apse **10** is also marked by two monumental trilithons.

In all, the area gives access to four doorways, each leading into another part of the temple compound.

The first entrance, the 'oculus entrance' on the primary axis, is the more conspicuous because of its

Large stone bowl, originally carved from a single stone. The surrounding walls show signs of extensive burning

Decorative stone screen with spiral composition

Tarxien Central. View of interior with spiral decorated screens and niches. A small hearth can be seen in the middle of the central passageway. The position of this heart suggests that only the apses may have been originally covered. In addition to providing access, the passageways also served as open courtyards or open spaces through which light and fresh air could enter the temple's rooms

location and design. Once over this barrier, apses **15** and **16**, visitors encounter a typical temple building following a symmetrical arrangements of apses. The first two apses beyond the 'oculus barrier' are separated by a passageway which also serves as a small court. The remains of a hearth stands in the middle of the courtyard, **14**. The apses, which are also well-built and exhibit the same detailed attention used in the two outer apses, also comprise two elaborately carved screens, which are not visible from the outer areas of the temple. The decorations of the screens combine a number of techniques that are well known in Maltese prehistoric art. Each panel is defined by a carved boundary within which are four flat spirals placed in a symmetrical arrangement. At the centre, the panel is marked by a circle. At the edge, triangles separate the spirals. The flat spaces left between the designs is highlighted by pit-hole decoration.

The two innermost apses reflect a number of alterations. Access to the apses is marked by a lintel. The main axis is dominated by a niche which also helps to distinguish one apse from the other. The right-hand apse, **19,** experienced substantial alterations. Some of these may have taken place during prehistory, but a number of scholars also believe that the area may have been re-utilized during Roman times. The original wall of this apse was not recovered during excavations. The present one is a post-excavation reconstruction which utilizes megaliths on the face of the wall which now forms part of the inner apse of Tarxien East. This reconstruction was confirmed by recent excavations carried by the Museums Department. The reconstructed areas suggests that apse **19** may have served as an access point leading into Tarxien East. The creation of such doorways was not unusual, especially in those cases where temples were altered by the addition

of adjoining chambers or niches. A trench still marks the floor of this apse.

The accompanying apse, **18**, on the other side of the corridor, suggests that these inner spaces may have been intended to receive decorated screens. One of these, with unfinished decorations, still stands in its original place.

Leaving the central parts of the temple and returning to the paved transitory space, it is noticed that two doorways flanking the link between Tarxien South and Tarxien Central, give access to ancillary chambers. One of these, chamber **11**, is accessed through the western apse, precisely through one of the monumental trilithons. Although now having a reconstructed capstone, the trilithon entrance to chamber **11** still reflects the importance that had once been given to this area. Surprisingly, the interior of the chamber is not at all impressive. The walls were fashioned out as part of a remodelling exercise

when the elevated niche in Tarxien South was constructed. A number of shelve recesses, built of stone slabs, make up the chamber's interior furnishings. Once again, as in similar structures and recesses found elsewhere throughout Tarxien, these recesses were found to contain animal bones as well as horn cores.

Across the passage way that links Tarxien South with Tarxien Central lies another important chamber **13** which is, however, entered via the transitory apse **12**. The chamber has lost much of its former splendour. In plan, the chamber follows an L-shape. Access may have once been through a monumental trilithon which has unfortunately not survived. A narrow passage way leads into this small chamber which is dominated by two large megaliths on which are carved images of bulls and a sow. The images emphasize the persistent importance of farm animals in the iconography of the Tarxien art repertoire.

The external wall of Tarxien Central

IMAGES FROM THE NEOLITHIC: THE BULLS AND SOW CHAMBER

A secluded chamber was set aside and decorated with large images of bulls and a sow with suckling piglets. The images were carved on the large megaliths that form the south wall of the chamber. The images reflect the importance that was accorded to farm animals in the Neolithic economy

The fourth doorway leads out of Tarxien Central. At the extreme end of the transitory apse **12**, less than a metre away from the doorway lies an interesting pit, the result of the removal of a paving stone. The pit provides a good view of the size of the paving stones. Also visible at the bottom of the pit is a round stone roller which was originally lodged under the threshold megalith. The roller may have been left in this position after having been used to transport or position the threshold megalith into position. Just outside the doorway, a staircase stands in a recess between the walls of Tarxien Central and Tarxien East. Did these steps lead to an upper level of the temple?

A roller is still lodged under a megalith near the eastern entrance of Tarxien Central.

A flight of steps, located just outside the eastern entrance of Tarxien Central, mark a curious feature of buildings. Scholars often speculate about the possibility of an upper floor that may have once stood above the present ruins

TARXIEN EAST

According to current dating
information, Tarxien East is older
than Tarxien Central. Admittedly,
this data has its limitations and may
require re-interpetation. In particular,
the craftsmanship seen in Tarxien
East is very similar to that of Tarxien
Central, a factor which suggests that
the two buildings may have originally
belonged to a single construction
phase. However, the temple stands
out for its lack of refined interiors such

as those of the previous buildings. These may have been lost as a result of destruction. Apart from the fine masonry, the temple lacks paving slabs, the floor having originally consisted of *torba*. Here and there are signs of rock-cutting for ground levelling. Available evidence suggests that the temple also experienced a number of changes as a result of the wider remodelling that was taking place throughout the temple compound. One major alteration may have involved the two western apses, **21** and **23** of the building. Being adjacent to the inner apses of Tarxien Central, the alterations or developments involving this part of the building have been partially obscured by a modern post-excavation reconstruction. The wall itself is a modern reconstruction. Recent investigations suggest that this area may have been altered to form a link with the innermost eastern apse of Tarxien Central.

One of a number of conical stones found at Tarxien

THE TARXIEN TEMPLES

MEGALITHIC ART

The Tarxien temples are certainly the most spectacular of all the Maltese temples in terms of their art and internal embellishments. A few images stand out. Foremost among these is the image of the colossal figure which, although being the biggest, was certainly not the only statue to be found in the temple. Indeed, the Tarxien temples provide an interesting insight into the use of figurines and small statues. Most of these were found without a head. Other art forms comprised a series of animal carvings, all derived from well-known repertoires of farm animal subjects. In addition, the art of megalithic carvings also included a series of spiral decorations which came in a number of forms and styles. The impressive aspect of these spirals is the sense of well-ordered design and composition. Elsewhere in the prehistoric world, spiral designs tend to be more organic and irregular. For decades, scholars have been split as to the sources of Maltese prehistoric art. While links with the eastern Mediterranean, or with western Europe have been discounted, it would seem that the inspiration for Maltese prehistoric art is a product of the archipelago. Vague links have been suggested with Sicily and Sardinia, but such links are purely formal rather than substantial.

WHAT TOOK PLACE WITHIN THE TARXIEN TEMPLES?

The Tarxien temples were once centres around which small communities gathered. Admittedly, the real social significance of Tarxien, and other contemporary buildings, is now a matter of scholarly research and speculation. For instance, it is believed that such elaborate buildings as Tarxien were nothing but the product of a basic social need to create central focal points. Such central focal points would have served to establish political organization, religious thought, ideology, commerce, and exchange, as well as several other fundamental elements of human society.

The building of Malta's temples, in the megalithic version that we can now admire, first occurred around 3600 BC. But previous versions, possibly constructed of different materials, or even built on much smaller scales with smaller stones, may have once existed. Often, the prolonged use of these sites meant that newer structures would have required the demolition of older ones. Yet, in spite of generations of change and development, the monuments ensured that that sense of space that originally characterized the location of the pre-temple settlements would have been retained. The use of robust megaliths ensured this.

A stone bead found close to the main entrance of Tarxien South

The energy and manpower required to build a temple compound such as that of Tarxien is an indication of the importance that was accorded to these buildings. The elaborate planning and beautiful carvings that embellished interiors stress the social standing of the buildings. Given that, during the Late Neolithic, burials took place in cemeteries such as that of the Hal Saflieni Hypogeum, it is highly unlikely that the buildings were related to burials. Excavations have to a large extent confirmed this. The Tarxien temples suggest that at least the image of a known personage (spiritual / deity or living dignitary) was given prominence and a level of respect that could have involved ritual or ceremonial activity. This possibility is strengthened by the presence of the colossal statue at Tarxien South. Other much smaller statues, some closely following the style of the colossal statue, were found in various chambers of the Tarxien temples.

Then there is the hollow decorated altar from Tarxien South which was found to contain a flint knife as well as the charred remains of animal bones. Such remains are reminiscent of rituals and ceremonies that are normally associated with sacrifices. In addition, several recesses in many of the chambers of the Tarxien temple compound were found to contain stacks of animal bones and horn cores.

A pair of beautifully-carved stone blocks were found at the back of apse 3 of the Tarxien South. The longest of these stone blocks, on the right, shows a procession of 22 horned goats

In spite of this, however, archaeology has yielded next to no clues as to the precise nature of the religion that was once practised in prehistoric Malta. Indeed, the use of the term 'temple' to denote Malta's megalithic buildings, is used rather generically owing no doubt to received wisdom, rather than to established certainties. The megaliths could have been given another label in recognition of their multi-use and purpose. Religion, ideology, and socio-economic factors may have easily coincided in the real functions of the Tarxien temples and its contemporary centres.

Part of a beautifully-carved stone found, together with the slab below, at the back of apse 3 of Tarxien South. The animals depicted on the stone are a ram and a pig followed by four goats.

Human head, stone

The complex design and layout of Tarxien may be a reflection of the social complexities that marked the archipelago's communities. The differentiation that so often marks society may have well been reflected in the careful planning and differentiation of the temple interiors. Indeed, even in their current state, the buildings are very suggestive of the way that they once exuded differentiation. The buildings may have been constructed from the fruits of collective endeavours, but their design and distinct structural elements encouraged distinctions between

Left: Small stone head, found in room 15, Tarxien Central

Above and below: Spiral decorated megaliths from Tarxien South

internal and external spaces, and even between spaces created within the interior arrangements themselves.

If we cannot say precisely what the specific functions of the Maltese megaliths were, we can at least get a glimpse of the worldview of the people who built them. Tarxien offers a window into a world that appears to be both familar and strange to the modern eye. The art objects found by Sir Temi Zammit are particularly interesting. Among the more eye-catching elements of these, are the numerous headless figurines and statues that were found at Tarxien. The image of these figurines may now be strange, almost sinister. But their function may have been of a more mundane nature. The statues may have served as votive offerings or mementos. Then there is the iconography of the carvings found within the Tarxien compound. These carvings show the importance that was given to animals, particularly farm animals. Images of bulls, sows,

pigs, sheep, and rams dominate this iconography. These animals would have provided the primary source of food and relate secondary products and, as such, they would have been valuable resources. These carved images may have also served as a display of wealth. The control measures within the temples may in turn be a reflection of the control of food resources. As social magnets, the temples may have exerted influence on food production and distribution, but evidence for this is lacking. Unknowingly to the craftsmen that produced them, the Tarxien carvings were to provide rare snapshot images of the very elements of a Neoltihic lifestyle. But the craftsmen were also accomplished in depicting abstract forms. The spiral remains one of the more important icons of prehistoric Malta. Its derivative designs, spread here and there across megaliths, remind us of images that may have been derived from nature.

An unusual carving in alabaster-like material

THE TARXIEN TEMPLES

TARXIEN AND THE END OF THE TEMPLE PERIOD

During the earlier months of his excavation campaigns at Tarxien, Sir Temi Zammit discovered an extensive cremation cemetery. The cemetery, which was dated to the Early Bronze Age, suddenly presented an as yet unexpected facet of Maltese prehistory. Among the major areas of scholarly debate, the cemetery raised questions as to how the temple period had come to and end. The demise of the temple period has traditionally been portrayed as having been a sudden event. Very few 'sudden events' have been adequately recorded in archaeology. The best examples are those related to volcanic eruptions that buried towns or cities, such as the prehistoric town of Akrotiri on the Aegean island of Thera (1600 BC) or the Roman city of Pompeii (79 AD). Although the prospect of a natural calamity cannot be ruled out, and evidence for such an event may yet come to light, the idea of a natural disaster has not yet been substantiated.

Nevertheless, the end of an era always elicits questions regarding the cause and effect of change. The Tarxien cremation deposit was found to rest on top of temple period deposits, and contained within the precincts of the buildings. According to Zammit, the cremation deposit was found to rest on debris that covered the chambers of the temples. The discovery of small metal daggers and axis, fuelled images of weapon-wielding intruders who dispatched the peaceful inhabitants of the islands. The burn marks on many of the Tarxien megaliths has often been indicated as evidence of this destructive event. In this scenario, the intruders are almost presented as a military force that wrecked havoc across the entire island and massacred the whole population of the archipelago.

General view of the Tarxien temples, from the east

Burn marks on some of the monoliths

Catastrophe theories come in various forms and versions. A variation on the theme of the arrival of foreigners sees newcomers arriving to find a deserted archipelago. The steady decrease of a small island population can be triggered by several causes. Small Mediterranean islands can be susceptible to extreme weather conditions, such as droughts and long dry seasons, that would have had a heavy burden on livestock and crops. Demographic growth in the Maltese islands has, in historical times, created pressures that required the importation of food and grain from Sicily. The carrying capacity of the Maltese islands, as well as the type of agriculture that may have been practised during the temple period, may have become dangerous factors in hard times. Bad time economics in an island society may not have offered too many alternatives to survival. The sudden loss of animal food resources, coupled with a series of bad harvests, would have been a likely cause of famine. Variations on the theme of catastrophes include social unrest created by the overpowering presence of the temples, disease, as well as intra-community conflict among others. Was the temple culture too isolated to allow an optimum survival and development of society? Was there hierarchical strife? What types of diseases or genetic problems would have played havoc in such a closed community?

Yet again, the demise of the temple period may have been nothing more than a mixture of social and cultural changes, where the old and the new blend into each other. Such is the evolution of history and society. The challenge, therefore, would be that of distinguishing between elements of continuity and elements of change, and to understand the processes and agency behind them.

RECONSTRUCTED TEMPLE FAÇADE?

Prehistoric models of contemporary builds are a unique feature of Maltese prehistoric antiquities. The illustrated fragments of an architectural model were discovered by sir Temi Zammit at Tarxien, and reconstructed by Luigi Maria Ugolini in 1936. Scholars still speculate about the accuracy of several aspects of the illustrated reconstructions. Equally significant is the importance that appears to have been attached to creating representations of well-known communal buildings. Architecture exerted an influence not only in the geographical sense but also on the visual culture of the prehistoric inhabitants of the Maltese islands.

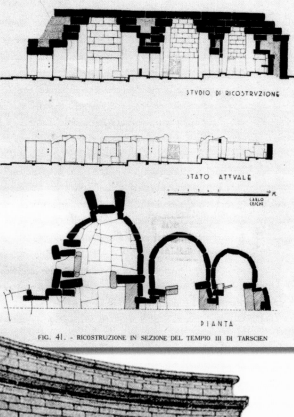

STVDIO DI RICOSTRVZIONE

STATO ATTVALE

PIANTA

FIG. 41. - RICOSTRUZIONE IN SEZIONE DEL TEMPIO III DI TARSCIEN

SIR TEMI ZAMMIT AND THE TARXIEN TEMPLES

The excavation of the Tarxien temples by Sir Themistocles Zammit (1864-1935) was an epoch-making event that put Malta on the world map of archaeology. Revered as the father of Maltese archaeology, Zammit became a distinguished researcher and practitioner in a number of different fields. Zammit first pursued a brilliant career as a medical practitioner, university professor, and senior government analyst in the Department of Health. These positions culminated in his discovery in the summer of 1905 which explained how undulant fever (Malta fever) was transmitted. Throughout this period, he laid the foundations of Maltese museology and archaeology, making impressive achievements in these sectors. Zammit established the first museum of archaeology and pursued an extensive career exploring the Maltese landscape apart from undertaking three decades of excavation projects. Zammit's pioneering work in landscape archaeology focused on the renowned cart-ruts. His excavations included work at the Hal Saflieni Hypogeum, the Tarxien temples, Ta' Hagrat, the Ghajn Tuffieha Roman Baths, as well as numerous Phoenician-Punic tombs. Zammit was the first to provide a sound framework for the chronology of Maltese antiquities. Zammit left the medical field to take up the position of rector at the University of Malta. In 1920 Zammit decided to focus entirely on the study of Maltese antiquities and, in 1926, he resigned as university rector. Zammit was a prolific writer, publishing important works in the field of archaeology, education, literature, medicine, public health, and Maltese history.

Sir Temi Zammit will be remembered for his epoch-making excavations of the Tarxien temples. The publication of these excavations made an impact on the world of scholarship. Overnight, the wonders of Malta's megalithic architecture and art were placed on the same international level as that traditionally occupied by Stonehenge and Minoan Crete. Zammit humbly took his place along such pioneering archaeologists as Sir Arthur Evans, a contemporary. The discovery of Tarxien afforded a unique opportunity for Zammit to examine a hitherto unexcavated temple. The results were breathtaking. Not only did Zammit excavate a prehistoric building, but he also unearthed one of the most important repertoires of ancient art works known from world prehistory as well as the famous colossal statue which has been hailed as the oldest monumental human representation known to date. Equally significant was Zammit's discovery of the Early Bronze cremation cemetery. This discovery served not only to link Maltese prehistory with the ancient world of metals but, even more importantly, it served to emphasize the antiquity of the Maltese temples.

TARXIEN AND THE EARLY BRONZE AGE

At Tarxien, Zammit found that various areas of the existing megalithic structure had been turned into a cremation cemetery. The cemetery consisted of a grey ashy deposit which contained a number of cremated human remains. Burials took place in urns, which were in turn accompanied by funerary gifts. These consisted mainly of ceramic vessels, personal ornaments and, in some special cases, copper axes and daggers.

These discoveries presented quite a contrast to the temple period custom of collective inhumations in underground tombs and cemeteries, such as those found at Xemxija and the Ħal Saflieni Hypogeum. The Tarxien temples may have provided a convenient group of large enclosures that could be used to accommodate pyres and burials.

The use of existing megaliths during the Early Bronze Age was a widespread phenomenon. The presence of Early Bronze Age pottery has been recorded at almost every known temple period building. Grey deposits, not necessarily containing cremated burials, have been noted at Tal-Qadi and the Xagħra Circle. The presence of the Tarxien Cemetery culture was therefore ubiquitous.

The discovery of copper axes and daggers at Tarxien technically meant

**Early Bronze Age
figurine from Tarxien**

an end of the stone-using technology in the form that had been known from previous centuries. The new styles of pottery and the introduction of new burial customs marked another aspect of change and innovation. Can these changes be adequately explained?

By the third millennium BC, metallurgy gained more prominence in terms of social significance. The indisputable increase in the use and circulation of copper and bronze objects has been characterized as a turning point in world prehistory. Symbols, customs, and traditions are thought to have experienced gradual but steady change as cultural values and new economic activities were being transformed. Although agriculture and the basic economic forces established during most

the Neolithic period persisted, a new social order began to emerge with new elements of prestige and hierarchy. In this new world order, social exchange, commerce, and regional interaction appear to have accelerated. In the Mediterranean, maritime activity and the emergence of polities began to gain in importance. It is thought that new exchange systems involving the circulation of prestigious objects made of bronze, gold, ceramic, and other materials, among leading communities and major village settlements, became a hallmark of such inter-regional activity. It is the scale of such activity that was to transform the Mediterranean.

It is difficult to say exactly when and how these broad regional developments began to leave an

Small geometrically-designed vases were a primary feature of cremation rituals.

impact on the Maltese islands. The Tarxien temples do, however, provide a few insights into this aspect of culture change. In this regard, the interesting subject of foreign contacts becomes a useful point of departure. A few particular objects found at Tarxien provide a sense of regional interaction, especially with the Aegean world, which was already a thriving centre of metallurgy by the third millennium BC. These contacts may have in all probability occurred via Sicily and South Italy. Such contacts also seem to have began during the temple period. A very distinctive type of pottery, often associated with a type of pottery known from the island of Thermi in the north-east Aegean, was unearthed in Late Neolithic contexts. We know from the Tarxien Cemetery that many attributes found in Early Bronze Age pottery figurines could have reflected a tradition that originated in Early and Middle Helladic Greece as well as Sicily and Capo Graziano on Lipari. Obsidian

was still arriving in Maltese islands. Tarxien provides one valuable clue of long-range regional interaction – the bossed bone plaque. These strange objects are very distinctive in design and appearance. Examples have been found in south-east Sicily, South Italy, Greece, and Troy.

In this new world order, the age of grand megalithic buildings slowly faded away. This is not to say that the fascination with monuments disappeared. The dolmen, a small megalithic monument that could be built with fewer resources, spread across the archipelago. But the age of communal construction projects had passed out of fashion. The Bronze Age may have therefore seen a shift in emphasis from highly-localized interests to broader external interaction. In this, the islands were responding to forces that would in later centuries bring the Maltese islands out of isolation and into the orbit of the Mediterranean powers of Archaic and Classical antiquity.

The small fragment of the bossed bone plaque represents the widening contacts that the Maltese islands enjoyed during the Early Bronze Age. The bone plaques are known from as far away as Troy and mainland Greece. The strange objects also circulated in Sicily and the south of Italy

Copper daggers and chisels buried along with cremated bodies may have represented new values or symbols of wealth and status

UNESCO WORLD HERITAGE

The Tarxien Temples are important monuments that have an important place in the history of world architecture. The significance of the temples is reflected in their design and construction methods, as well as their role in the shaping of society. The importance of the Tarxien temple complex also lies in its scientific value. Throughout evolution, monuments and other elements of material culture were created out of the sheer inventiveness and creativity that has distinguished humankind from other beings. The Tarxien temples, along with other singular heritage monuments know from around the world, are reminders of this phenomenon. The uniqueness of the Tarxien megaliths has earned them an undisputed place on the UNESCO World Heritage List.